D0360088

SAVED FROM SUCCESS

SAVED FROM SUCCESS

How God Can Free You from Culture's Distortion of Family, Work, and the Good Life

DALE PARTRIDGE

An Imprint of Thomas Nelson

Published in Nashville, Tennessee, by Nelson Books, an imprint of Thomas Nelson. Nelson Books and Thomas Nelson are registered trademarks of HarperCollins Christian Publishing, Inc.

The author is represented by the Christopher Ferebee Agency, www.christopherferebee.com.

Thomas Nelson titles may be purchased in bulk for educational, business, fund-raising, or sales promotional use. For information, please e-mail SpecialMarkets@ThomasNelson.com.

ISBN 978-0-7180-9345-7 (eBook)

Library of Congress Cataloging-in-Publication Data

Library of Congress Control Number: 2018932496
ISBN 978-0-7180-9344-0

Printed in the United States of America

18 19 20 21 22 LSC 10 9 8 7 6 5 4 3 2 1

To my sons, Honor and Valor, may this book remind you of your father's heart regarding right and wrong, good and evil, and winning and losing. May these pages cause you to stand for God's Truth—whatever the cost.

Contents

"For My thoughts are not your thoughts,
Nor are your ways My ways," says the Lord.
"For as the heavens are higher than the earth,
So are My ways higher than your ways,
And My thoughts than your thoughts."

Isaiah 55:8–9

Critical Introduction

Can someone believe in Jesus and not be a Christian?

Sure. The book of James says, "Even the demons believe—and tremble!" (2:19). So what makes someone a Christian?

In the book of Romans, Paul tells us, "if you confess with your mouth the Lord Jesus and believe in your heart that God has raised Him from the dead, you will be saved" (10:9).

The key phrase we must examine here is "confess with your mouth." Does Paul simply want us to say the words *Lord Jesus* out loud in the public square? Not exactly.

The word *confess* means to authentically acknowledge something with conviction.

In other words, Paul is saying that if we authentically acknowledge that Jesus is the Lord of our lives and we believe that God has raised Jesus from the dead, then, and only then, will we receive the eternal gifts associated with Christianity.

However, lordship is where most people withdraw. They want Jesus the Savior. They want heaven. They want the fruits of the faith. But they don't want a Lord.

Let me offer you an example to explain what I mean: "Savior" is something Jesus does for us, but it's not who He is. To explain, I'll use an example from my life. My wife cleans the house for me and she does it well. But she's not my housekeeper; she's my wife. Furthermore, she only cleans our house because she's my wife. If I reduced her to simply "housekeeper," not only would we have serious problems but it would also strip her of who she truly is in my life.

The same is true with Jesus. While He *saves* us from God's wrath, minimizing Him to that solitary role while ignoring His true position of Lord is not just insulting; it's make believe. That is to say, Jesus can't save what is not His; and if you refuse to release the deed to your life, then there is nothing to rescue.

I think this concept is best illustrated in Matthew 16:25 where Jesus says, "For whoever desires to save his

To call yourself a follower of Christ, you must be willing to relinquish the authority of your life to Him. You must allow His cross to do its deadly work to your flesh.

—DALE PARTRIDGE

life will lose it, but whoever loses his life for My sake will find it."

To call yourself a follower of Christ, you must be willing to relinquish the authority of your life to Him. You must allow His cross to do its deadly work to your flesh. You must be willing to yield your heart to His commandments. But most of all, you must surrender your way for His way.

I tell you this for one reason: this book is for Christians. This book is for people willing to submit their perspective to God's ways regardless of how unpopular they may be to the culture or how uncomfortable they might be to your flesh.

This book is for people who are tired of doing life *their* way. This book is for people who are ready to surrender. There is no path faster than God's path. There is no path more profitable than God's path. There is no path more enjoyable than God's path. This book is for people who only want that path.

Succeeding at Failing

"I'm going to be a millionaire by the time I turn thirty."

It was a bold declaration for an eighteen-year-old to make to his dad, but I've never been timid. Plus, I believed every word.

Just three months prior, I watched my parents go through a vicious divorce that left our family in financial chaos, which meant I had to make my own way, and fast. I had just graduated high school in a small town in Southern California and was striking out on my own, determined to "make it." I walked out of my dad's house that day and dove headfirst into the real world with nothing to guide me except my brokenness and culture's definition of success.

The years between eighteen and twenty-four sped past in a blur. I worked eighteen-hour days and almost never took time off. I didn't backpack across Europe. I didn't road trip with friends. To be honest, I don't think I had one overnight trip in a four-year span. All I did was . . . work. I launched a fitness company and a rock-climbing gym, a conference organization and an advertising agency. I even wrote and self-published a book.

My intensity and fanaticism did not go unnoticed. Money started rolling in, and the only thing that outpaced my salary was my lifestyle. I leased cars I couldn't afford and had parties bigger than my paycheck could finance. I even remember applying for a Best Buy credit card to purchase a ridiculous television that I "needed."

Even writing this, it seems gross. However, I was a respectful young man. I was polite, disciplined, responsible, and a Christian (which I later realized made it difficult for those close to me to critique my lifestyle). Nevertheless, everywhere I turned people commented about how I was "going places" and how I "had what it takes." Friends and family members expressed their pride and cheered me on. It became a perfect storm of affirmation that dialed up my drive, pushing me to perform harder and pursue more.

What God Said.

How I Lived.

At age twenty-six, for the first time in my career, I began to feel the tension between what God said and how I lived in terms of money. Months later, I founded a socially conscious company called Sevenly, which donated a portion of its sales to good causes. In hindsight, my intentions were good; however, it was simply me slapping a big *GOD* sticker on my company in hopes of further validating my desperate need for approval from the moral community. And my subconscious strategy worked. Sevenly exploded to nearly fifty employees rushing around a gorgeous office in downtown Orange County just ten minutes from the beach. We generated hundreds of thousands in revenue each week, once even hitting a million dollars in a seven-day stretch.

Sevenly's success put me on the map in the world of entrepreneurship. I landed on the cover of *Entrepreneur* magazine and on the front page of the *Los Angeles Times*. I was featured on national television and radio programs. My name appeared on every "40 under 40" and "30 under 30" list in the marketplace. Jack Dorsey, the cofounder of Twitter and founder of Square, personally invited me to have a private lunch with him at his headquarters in downtown San Francisco. Then came Adobe, Panasonic, and Chick-fil-A, and even Facebook invited me to deliver a keynote presentation. I was the opening talk before

Mark Zuckerberg's address at their private conference celebrating the social network's tenth anniversary.

I was the picture of success. At least according to culture's definition. I raked in a heavy six-figure salary, owned two homes, and drove luxury cars. My wife was a model, and my business was growing. People knew me and wanted to be like me. I had money, influence, and fame.

But on the inside, I was a wreck.

If you had asked me whether my life was fulfilling at the height of my "success," I wouldn't have hesitated: "Of course," I would have said, because I assumed that was what being fulfilled felt like. We only know what we've been taught, what we've seen, and what's been modeled for us. Sure, I had some issues, but what successful person doesn't? I was achieving everything the culture around me said was important.

I was burnt out and overstimulated, but I was generating great financial returns. My friendships felt strained, but hey, my social media following had skyrocketed. I didn't take time to relax; I'd have plenty of time to improve my work-life balance when I got older. My spiritual life had been reduced to scanning the daily Scripture verse on my phone's Bible app, but I wasn't a minister. I was an entrepreneur.

By 2014 I was drowning in success and my health was paying the price. Without warning, panic attacks would pounce on me, leaving me shivering midday in my bedroom. Insomnia had me wandering the halls of my house in the early hours of the morning. Over time, strange manifestations of stress emerged: rapid heart palpitations, stabbing stomach pain, and mysterious nerve twitches in my calves and cheeks. I rushed to the emergency room every few months for fear that I was dying.

The poor health of my professional life bled into my home life. I had married a wonderful woman in 2010, but our marriage was a disaster. I wasn't leading, and she had no one to follow. An unrelenting pressure descended on our house every time I walked through the front door and dragged my office stress in with me. In the evenings we would often sit just a few feet away from each other but felt miles apart. We were close, but we weren't connected. Women have a strong sense of intuition, and Veronica is no exception. She knew that her emotional protection, my health, and our spiritual well-being were not my priority. As a result, we lived like roommates playing house who shared a bed yet lived independent lives.

My life was constructed of toothpicks, and it finally

CULTURE SAYS:

~~Impressing the world is the currency of success.~~

GOD HAS TAUGHT ME:

Seek My approval and your best life will follow.

collapsed on April 9, 2014, when a member of Sevenly's board informed me that I was being fired from my own company. Due to a recent algorithm change in how Facebook presented information, the company's growth had slowed dramatically. But more than that, I was informed of my blindness. My staff had turned against me. I lost their trust. I lost their respect. Ultimately, my pace of life and my prideful persona had caught me by the shirt and ripped it straight off my back.

There I stood, a few months shy of my thirtieth birthday. A millionaire. A broken, empty, miserable millionaire. I had lived up to the promise I'd made to my father twelve years earlier, but it had cost me more than I ever imagined. I thought I was succeeding at success, but I was actually succeeding at failing.

Bumping Into Truth

Someone once told me that there's no feeling more depressing than climbing the ladder of success only to realize that you're on top of the wrong building. I realized how true that is after I was fired from Sevenly. Over the next year, I was brought low. Awkwardly, painfully, humiliatingly low. I tried to hide it. To justify it. To spin it. To ignore it. In every possible way I was running from it. But I knew I needed to make some serious changes in my life. It was like I was withdrawing from a drug. I had been addicted to culture's definition of success, and I was in desperate need of rehab.

Veronica and I realized we needed a new start, so we sold our homes, packed up, and moved our family to a small town in central Oregon. The pace was slower, the traffic lighter, the air fresher. I felt confident that I had made the right decision for our family.

Shortly after arriving, Veronica and I had a fight. We were sitting upstairs in the tiny apartment we were renting, but the conversation made me feel as if we were back in our house in Orange County. She was crying over what seemed to be a relapse into my previous behavior and unreasonable work schedule. I argued, "I'm so close to creating the dream we've been talking about. Slowing down doesn't make sense right now." And at that exact moment—*ding!*—I received a text message from a pastor whom I hadn't spoken with in months. It read, "Dale, God wanted me to tell you this: 'Dale, I love you and I am for you. Your dreams will happen by My strength.'"

Like a wave of love crashing over my soul, I immediately broke down in tears. The timing was too precise

God.

Me.

not to be divine. Veronica wept as well. We realized that the God of the universe was literally listening to our conversation. This faith we had and this Jesus whom we followed were real, and in that moment, we genuinely started our new lives.

Just a few weeks later, I attended a birthday party for my friend's son. That's where I met Matt, a six-foot-three, gray-haired guy with eight kids. From the moment we first spoke, I realized Matt had a level of calm and maturity I'd never encountered before. He was kind and compassionate, embracing me just as I was, but he also was honest in speaking the truth. He had an extraordinary family, a thriving marriage, and a level of spiritual authority beyond any Christian I had known.

I'd had several mentors since deciding to follow Jesus twelve years earlier. I had even spent time with renowned counselors, coaches, and pastors. But I had never been *discipled* by someone until I met Matt. Together, we began to think critically about what success meant. From family and marriage to money and maturity, I began unlearning and relearning what the Christian life was intended to look like.

One of the first questions he asked me was about the Bible. Did I believe it was "the Word of God"? I wasn't sure what he meant, so he asked it another way.

"Is your heart yielded to the Scriptures or do you simply have a smorgasbord approach to your faith?"

I'd never heard the phrase "smorgasbord approach," but it wasn't long before I realized that's exactly how I was living. I took the Bible seriously only when I understood it or when it made sense to my emotions, but I ignored its commands in those areas that were culturally costly or difficult to swallow. Ultimately, the way I was living wasn't consistently matching up to the way God instructs us to live.

So it began. Over the coming months we met almost daily. Whenever I would begin reverting to my previous view of success, he would place a passage of Scripture before me and say, "Here's what the Bible says on that. Now what are you going to do about it?"

Over time, through the power of the Holy Spirit, I began to transform my thoughts from cultural to Christian. I learned that who I come home to is more important than the house I come home to. I learned that people are more impactful than places. I learned that God's approval was more significant than earthly fame. I learned that money isn't the measure of my worth.

Matt lived by the slogan "If you believe wrong, you'll never live strong." In other words, the way we think determines the paths we take. And I was thinking unbiblically. I had accepted lies as truth.

Our mind-sets and our results are deeply connected. Because many leaders today have a broken view of success, they live broken lives. I was one of these leaders. But through my relationship with Matt, I began to redefine the terms I'd been living by. I was saved from "success."

Popular, Meet Superior

Before we dive in, let's perform a little thought experiment. Close your eyes for a minute and imagine that you're continuing down your current path with your current definition of success. You keep working as hard as you're working. And you keep prioritizing the things you're prioritizing. And you keep experiencing the strains that are weighing you down. What will your life look like in three to five years? Will your relationship with your spouse be stagnant or thriving? Will your connections with your children be healthy or hollow? What will be the state of your mental and physical health? And what about your relationship with God?

If you're anything like I was, imagining your future can be underwhelming at best.

Most Christians don't know they're on the wrong road. Most of us have good intentions for prosperity and wealth and influence, but deep down we know our hearts have veered slightly off track. We somehow forget that our small detours from God's way of living become big canyons in the not-so-distant future. We fail to remember that a little bit of the world's way can prevent us from His way. For many of us it's not on purpose. It's a slow fade—like a lobster in warm water too oblivious to realize he's being cooked. The trick is waking up, turning back, and moving Godward.

The world's definition of *success* according to the Oxford dictionary is: "the attainment of popularity or profit."[1] The thesaurus's list of synonyms includes *prosperity*, *affluence*, *wealth*, *fame*, *reward*, and *opulence*.[2] While most of us might not admit that our definition is this shallow, the things we devote our lives to tell a different story. My journey has taught me something important: a fish doesn't know it's wet.

So what if I told you that success is the opposite of what you have been taught? What if I showed you that everything you believe about achievement and fulfillment is faulty? What if I said that you've spent your life pursuing a lie that will only lead to disappointment? Would you be offended? Would you reject my suggestion as wrong?

The older I get and the longer I live, the more I realize that culture's way of success is simply foolishness. That the direction of the majority is actually the opposite of maturity. That what is popular is almost never superior, and trendy does not equal better.

The world's "advice" will often take more than you're willing to give and leave you in a worse place than you started. For example, most people are in debt, most people watch television, most people look at pornography, most people work for someone else, most people don't have a retirement plan, most people get divorced, and most people rent their homes rather than own them.

Do you want to be like most people? Me neither.

One of the wisest men who ever lived, the apostle Paul, once wrote, "Let no one deceive himself. If anyone among you seems to be wise in this age, let him become a fool that he may become wise. For the wisdom of this world is foolishness with God."[3]

Veronica and I have always been extremely cautious about doing "what most people do." In our experience, when we see a metaphorical crowd, we stop and ask, "Why is everyone running over there?"

Most people are fighting for a vision of success that, in reality, is a failure. Most think their notions of success are rooted in wisdom when they're actually rooted in folly. Most people are straining to be rich and famous but have ended up relationally and morally bankrupt. Most people don't even think twice. Most people just chase what everyone else chases. Most people desire what the media and culture have taught them to desire. In turn, most people create the same life everyone else creates.

Interestingly, this isn't my idea. The Bible clearly warns us about the risks involved in a life lived inside the majority. Jesus told us in Matthew 7:13–14, "Enter by the narrow gate; for wide is the gate and broad is the way that leads to destruction, and there are *many* who go in by it. Because narrow is the gate and difficult is the way which leads to life, and there are few who find it" (emphasis added).

Convinced yet? You may be thinking, *Dale, I'm a Christian and I follow Jesus. I go to church and I already understand what's right and wrong. How does this apply to me?* The Bible says, "Take heed lest [you] fall."[4] Sadly, Christians are not exempt from this cultural-success disease. Some may be creative at sanitizing their actions to appear holy, but in my experience, many if not most church-going Christians have been infected with this counterfeit definition of success deep in their bones.

Ultimately, you don't have to be like most people. You can choose to go right when everyone runs left. You can cultivate a deeper and more fulfilling life by embracing a biblical way of thinking and living. What this world calls "the smart direction" isn't the right direction. What is trendy or common is actually foolish and unwise.

True success is often counterintuitive to how our culture defines it. In other words, being weak is strong. Being quiet is loud. And being last is first. In the pages that follow, I want to take you on the journey I started years ago under Matt's discipleship. To challenge what you've come to believe success looks like. To put the Scriptures before you and say, "Here is what the Bible says. Now what are you going to do about it?"

True success is waiting for us all. It's just not in the place where *most people* seek it.

01

Marriage

Veronica and I see it all the time. A thirty-two-year-old boy who has been dating a beautiful woman for five years or more. The couple has talked about marriage, but they aren't making wedding plans. If you ask them why they aren't ready to make the commitment, they'll tell you, "We need more time to figure out life" or "We still need to work on us." But if you get real deep, they'll likely tell you they aren't sure if their significant other is "the one." It's as if five years wasn't enough time to gather the proper information to know whether the other person would make an acceptable spouse.

Do you know a couple like this? Statistically speaking, you probably do because the average age of marriage in America has been steadily climbing. In the 1960s, the average age of marriage for both men and women was their early twenties. Now the average age of marriage for men in America is twenty-nine and for women it is twenty-seven.[1] Meanwhile, the marriage rate itself is declining. In other words, fewer people are marrying, and those who are getting married are doing so much later.

To make the battle even more difficult, culture (even Christian culture) encourages delayed marriage and celebrates the benefits of waiting to wed. If you get married later, "you'll have more time for education" or "you'll earn more money," and you'll have more time to discover the ultimate Holy Grail: "your true self." I saw an article recently, titled "Finding Yourself Before You Find 'The One.'" A related article was titled "Find Yourself Before You Find Love."

Have you ever looked for this idea in the Bible? You won't find it. In fact, you won't find this concept in any literature before the modern era. It is a relatively new idea. It's trendy. And it's unsafe thinking.

The Bible's teaching on marriage is unambiguous: "It is *not good* that man should be alone."[2] That wasn't spoken by Abraham or Moses or the apostle Paul. It was spoken by God, and it forms the foundation of our understanding of marriage as Christians. Some have refuted this verse as God merely stating it is "not good" for Adam to be alone on the earth. In other words, the passage is simply calling for more humans, not a wife. I disagree. As we see in the scriptures, God doesn't make him another human. He makes Adam a wife and just five verses later leaves us with the infamous, "Therefore a man shall leave his father and mother and be joined to his *wife*, and they shall become one flesh. And they were both naked, the man and his *wife*, and were not ashamed."[3]

Furthermore, we cannot think that Adam was lonely because he was imperfect. Adam was lonely because he was perfect. Sin had not yet entered the world and even still, God says an unmarried man left by himself is "not good." This proves that marriage isn't some necessary union because of our sin. This proves that even in a perfect world, with two perfect humans, marriage is what God desires.

I appreciate the thoughts of theologian Albert Mohler, who has made a case for getting married sooner rather than later:

> The vast majority of Christians who have gone before us would surely be shocked by the very need for a case to be made for Christian adults to marry. . . .

> Our bodies are not evolutionary accidents, and God reveals his intention for humanity through the gifts of sexual maturation, fertility, and sexual desire. As men and women, we are made for marriage. As Christians, those not called to celibacy are called to demonstrate our discipleship through honoring the Creator's intention by directing sexual desire and reproductive capacity into a commitment to marriage. Marriage is the central crucible for accepting and fulfilling the adult responsibilities of work, parenthood, and the full acceptance of maturity.[4]

But I can hear it now: "Paul was single!" and "Jesus was single!" which is true. But those statements, without bringing biblical identity to uphold them, put both Paul and Jesus at enmity with what God the Father has written and with what these men taught throughout the New Testament.

While many of you might rest on the "Jesus was single" argument, need I remind you of what the Bible is actually about? A marriage. A wedding between God's Son and His betrothed bride (the church). So yes, Jesus was single. But His death was a proposal, His resurrection was an engagement, and His return will be a wedding.

Yes, Jesus was single. But His death was a proposal, His resurrection was an engagement, and His return will be a wedding.

—DALE PARTRIDGE

But to put aside the complicated topic of righteous or unrighteous singleness, I want to make one thing clear: I am by no means shaming people for being single. I was single until I was twenty-four, and many of my respected friends were single through their early thirties. I understand the unique timeline God has for each person.

Nevertheless, more often than not, the "Paul was single" argument has been vandalized and impoverished of its truth by not adhering to the proper interpretation of his words found in 1 Corinthians 7:6–9:

> But I say this as a concession, not as a commandment. For I wish that all men were even as I myself. But each one has his own gift from God, one in this manner and another in that.
>
> But I say to the unmarried and to the widows: It is good for them if they remain even as I am; but if they cannot exercise self-control, let them marry. For it is better to marry than to burn with passion.

Paul's statement, in short, is this: "What I'm about to say is not divine doctrine but personal instruction. I really wish each of you had the gift of singleness for the purpose of full-time ministry as I do. That is, the gift to have complete self-control over my thoughts, actions, and physical desires. But if you do not have that gift and find the opposite sex sexually attractive or lustfully appealing, then it's better for you to get married."

Ultimately, ladies and gentlemen, if you have the natural desire for the opposite sex, you do not have the gift of singleness. Furthermore, if you're alleviating that desire in any way other than with your spouse, the Bible has labeled such activity fornication or adultery. Sure, you can attempt to justify secretive masturbation, but it's my understanding that sex with yourself is sex outside of marriage. If you don't agree, just be prepared to present your position at the throne. Moreover, it's our honest management of these natural sexual desires that should be the rocket fuel that propels us to finding our mate, not the private self-gratification that extends the search.

Having said that, the reason most people choose to continue waiting to get married has little to do with the authenticity of their "call to singleness" or even needing to make sure that they are with "the one." Instead, it is highly driven by fear and selfishness. As educated adults, we know that love requires sacrifice and that marriage is wonderful but also difficult. Yet we are intimidated by the sacrifices necessary for a healthy marriage.

CULTURE SAYS:

~~Find yourself before you find your spouse.~~

WHAT GOD HAS TAUGHT ME:

You find yourself through your spouse.

Others, especially men, are scared that marriage will limit them to only one woman for the rest of their lives, an idea I believe is simply not true. As for me, I fell in love with a nineteen-year-old rock climber, married a twenty-year-old animal lover, started a family with a twenty-four-year-old mother, built a farm with a twenty-five-year-old homemaker, and today I'm married to a twenty-eight-year-old woman of wisdom. If your mind is healthy, you'll never get tired of one woman or one man. You'll actually become overwhelmed with how many beautiful versions of your spouse you get to marry over the years.

Of course, once you're in a marriage, the work begins. We often fail to love our spouses well because we love ourselves supremely. A friend once told me, "Marriage isn't hard because we have to deal with the opposite sex. It's hard because it's the first time we must deal with ourselves." We see this truth when we have to confront the ways we have elevated our dreams, our career, our independence, and even our children above our spouse.

Sadly, I speak from experience. In 2011 life looked great from the outside. I was a good husband simply pursuing a passion. I was providing for my family and paving my own way. As I mentioned in the previous chapter, everybody was cheering me on: "Go, Dale!" and "Saw you on TV!" and "Love that you're doing so well."

Their ignorance was bliss. They fell prey to our culture's disgusting decline in relational responsibility. They saw one inch deep and believed it to be enough to validate the entirety of my story. But it wasn't. I wasn't okay. Veronica and I weren't okay. I was a man destroying my marriage through my business. I was a spiritually immature husband gaining the whole world while losing my wife.

While we don't have the time to indulge in all the details of our marriage's revival, I will tell you the solution occurred through the gentle rebukes of older, godly men not giving in to my excuses or manipulations. They forced me to face the reality of my commitments through the lens of God's Word and essentially allowed me to break my own heart with my own actions. The life I was living, regardless of how shiny it may have appeared, was in opposition to how the Bible had instructed me to live, to love, and to lead.

Along my journey to redefining success in marriage, I learned many things in regard to cherishing my wife and leading our family well. But one of the top lessons is that marriage is to be guarded. As Hebrews 13:4 says, "Let marriage be held in honor among all, and let the marriage bed be undefiled, for God will judge the sexually immoral and adulterous" (ESV). As Gary Thomas famously asked, "What if God designed marriage to make us holy more than to make us happy?"[5]

In relation to guarding our marriages, we must not ignore what might be the Enemy's chief strategy for the destruction of marriage: infidelity and adultery. One leads to the other, and the statistics are clear: 85 percent of these affairs begin at work.[6] As men and women of faith, we must stop pretending we're impervious to infidelity. Wiser, stronger, better couples have fallen before us.

So tomorrow, when you leave your home to build the business or the career that creates the life and security you desire for your family, be sure your spouse is confident in your love and commitment to your marriage. I can't tell you how many professionals are restrained from success because of the unaddressed insecurity of a spouse. There's nothing more powerful than a business leader with a spouse who can confidently cheer their lover's dreams toward the finish line. As a self-employed husband I must be proactive in the protection of the woman I claim to love. I must help her feel secure by making her my priority, showing her that I notice her and appreciate her, and reminding her of my faithfulness to our marriage. She must know that at work I am working diligently not only to produce wealth but to protect the relationship we've spent so much time developing.

While the workplace is one territory used by Satan, the unbiblical mind is his base camp. For some, he works through temptation; for the rest, he works through lies. In my experience there's a particular lie that almost every married person has had whispered in his or her ear: "You can do better." The idea that who you have is not enough. The idea that if you had married someone else you would fight less, hurt less, and love more. Or maybe the money would be different or the sex would be better or maybe your life would simply be easier.

However, God has taught me that maturity is never earned through the escape of something tough. It's earned through the commitment of remaining faithful in the face of struggle, even when it doesn't make sense to our flesh.

First Timothy 6:6 says, "Now godliness with contentment is great gain." The deeper meaning of this passage implies that contentment is a choice. And this leads to a weighty question: Do we trust that God's choice for our spouse is greater than our momentary dissatisfaction? Do we believe that God knows how to make good decisions on our behalf?

God has taught me that maturity is never earned through the escape of something tough. It's earned through the commitment of remaining faithful in the face of struggle, even when it doesn't make sense to our flesh.

—DALE PARTRIDGE

Now you might be thinking, *God didn't choose my spouse; I did.* You can believe that as long as you're willing to call Jesus a liar for His words in Mark 10:9: "Therefore what God has joined together, let not man separate." If you're struggling to know what God's choice is for your spouse, there is a solution. Just go into your closet, open your safe, take out your marriage license, and read it. More than once.

Furthermore, let us not forget the words of the apostle Peter: "Be sober, be vigilant; because your adversary the devil walks about like a roaring lion, seeking whom he may devour."[7] Marriages are under attack. The men and women who have not prepared for battle—with Scripture and self-control—will find that they are prey in a wilderness they can't escape.

Destroying or distorting marriage between a man and a woman is the enemy's ultimate opportunity to vandalize the visual representation of Christ and His bride. A reality which reveals something quite beautiful, God's intention for marriage is not merely a sacred covenant between man and woman. It is also to be the walking, talking, and living picture of Jesus and His Church. As a result, every divorce becomes a screaming endorsement to the world that says, "The Gospel will eventually fail you." Every Christian wife who commits adultery against her husband becomes a spiritual metaphor for the Church desiring a savior other than Jesus. Every Christian husband who compromises his devotion to his bride tells the world that Christ is not reliable. Consequently, broken marriages not only reduce the faith this world has in the Bible's great heavenly marriage to come, but they also achieve the exact opposite of God's desire for us.

In John 17:21 Jesus prays that God would move so "that they all may be one, as You, Father, are in Me, and I in You; that they also may be one in Us, that the world may believe that You sent Me."

Our unity, from the church to our marriages, is the means by which the world will know God sent Jesus. Our contentment with the spouse that God has given us is public evidence that Jesus, by Himself, is sufficient for all of our spiritual needs.

Ultimately, the Bible instructs husbands to "love your wives, just as Christ also loved the church."[8] It instructs wives to "submit to your own husbands, as to the Lord."[9] The symbolic parallels are glaring. But the Christian couple who has forgotten what their marriage represents in this broken culture is the couple who has advertised their own disbelief. But regardless of how unfaithful we are with His image in this world,

Our unity, from the church to our marriages, is the means by which the world will know God sent Jesus.

—DALE PARTRIDGE

we serve a God who prefers mercy. A God who always comes back. A God who remains faithful, even when we don't deserve it.

If you look at the world's most "successful" people, from CEO's and celebrities to professional athletes and musicians, a healthy marriage, or even the very concept of marriage, seems to be absent. Much of the population has followed suit. Millions have bought into the lie that a covenant relationship with a spouse will somehow slow you down, prevent your ability to reach your potential, and prolong the achievement of your goals.

However, the Bible stands in staunch opposition. The pages of God's truth reveal that marriage often speeds up the growth of one's character and maturity. It demonstrates that the practice of deep commitment strengthens our ability to accomplish God's purpose. But the ultimate thing the Bible tells us about marriage is that it exists for the glory of God. In other words, it exists to display God. To display the Gospel. To display the grand narrative of Scripture. This is why marriage exists. This why we should want marriage. This is why we should promote marriage. This is why marriage is so important to our success.

02

Children

I recently took my daughter Aria to a trampoline park in our hometown of Bend, Oregon. If you've never been to one, imagine a warehouse where most of the floor is made of stretchy polypropylene and filled with bouncing grade-schoolers. It's a magical place for kids, and apparently a nice retreat for parents who like to badmouth their children behind their backs.

As Aria was jumping, I slipped over to the parent corner where I could observe her in all areas of the park. There, I overheard parents having the type of negative conversations about their kids that have become typical in modern America. One in particular stuck with me.

"How far along are you?" a father asked a woman who was clearly pregnant.

"About six months," she groaned. "What am I thinking?"

They both laughed at her sarcasm.

"Yeah, most days being a parent is like being tortured, amirite?" he said.

"I know. I feel like I never get enough time with adults anymore," she replied.

"I feel you," he said, nodding his head.

"Yeah, this one was a total accident," she said, rubbing her pregnant belly, "but I guess we'll deal with it."

If you're a parent and you're honest, this isn't the first time you've encountered a conversation like this. Perhaps you've even participated in one.

Parents moan and groan and gripe and sigh and talk about how children make their lives so much more difficult. Of course, most parents love their children. And surely they would never utter such grumbles within earshot of their little ones. But this has become the language of our culture. This is how we talk about our children. No wonder we're having fewer children and are waiting longer to start families.

In a recent study, one-third of millennials say they do not want to have children. What are the top reasons for opting out? Thirty-four percent say they don't want to give up their flexibility. Thirty-two percent say they

CULTURE SAYS:

~~Children are an obstacle in the way of my lifestyle.~~

GOD HAS TAUGHT ME:

A lifestyle rejecting children is a lifestyle preventing maturity.

don't want to take on additional responsibilities. Some even say they don't want children because they love their sleep too much. As one researcher who worked on the study concluded, these trends are "indicative of their desire to construct their own personal paths to happiness."[1] Or maybe millennials have simply heard the conversations parents have been having and have taken note.

I encountered this same mind-set recently at a friend's dinner party. Over finger foods and hors d'oeuvres, I struck up a conversation with a guy and his wife. He told me that he and his bride had been married for a few years, and he served as a youth pastor at a local church, which I'd already guessed. The skinny jeans and high school slang were dead giveaways. But when I casually asked him if they had kids, his answer stunned me.

"No, man. We're waaaaaaaay too selfish for kids." His wife nodded and grinned. "But we got a puppy. So I guess we're practicing."

It was a perfect picture of the culture's understanding of children. That kids get in the way of what we want in life. That they impede us from achieving what is "truly" important. And this young adult minister—this man chosen by a church to set an example for young people on how the Bible should be lived out—was parroting the culture's view. No wonder so many millennials would rather buy a puppy than birth a child.

If you read what God says about children, it sounds nothing like our culture's attitude toward them. The psalmist wrote that children are a "heritage from the LORD" and "offspring a reward from him."[2] Solomon said that "children are a crown to the aged."[3] And Jesus was famous for elevating the status of children, which was especially significant considering that first-century Judaism often limited children's social status.

Dr. John Trainer said, "Children are not a distraction from the more important work. They are the most important work." Our culture will tell you that children will impede your dreams. But the Bible says that children should *be* the dream. Culture instructs us to wait as long as we can before having kids. The Bible implies in Genesis 1:28 that if you're not ready to have children, you may not be ready to be married. Simply put, to take deliberate, unnatural, and long-term measures to prevent what naturally occurs when a husband and wife become "one flesh" is to evade the very hope that God has for your togetherness—multiplication. Put another way: if you're not ready to follow God's command to multiply, are you actually ready to become one flesh?

“Children are not a distraction from the more important work. They are the most important work.”

—DR. JOHN TRAINER

Now, this is obviously an extrapolation of Scripture, however, it deserves our sincere contemplation. To be clear, I'm not condemning natural family planning. I am, though, challenging those who have decided that total prevention—especially prevention driven by fear, faithlessness, or selfishness—should be at least examined through prayer, Scripture, and deep spiritual evaluation. That being said, you might consider asking yourself how your life might look if you and your spouse yielded to a less calculated position on children. But most of all, I'm asking you to question if you're truly living as if children are blessings to your life or if they are simply being viewed as burdens you must lovingly embrace.

A related message from culture is that children should only be had in moderation. We speak of children like they're donuts: good so long as you don't have too many. But can you ever have too many blessings? Why would you want fewer rewards from God instead of more? Wealth is a blessing. Would you refuse more wealth? Wisdom is a blessing. Would you reject additional wisdom? Influence is a blessing. Would you decline further influence? So why have we detached children from this parallel logic?

The psalmist wrote, "Blessed is the man whose quiver is full of [children]."[4] If you are determined to have only 1.7 children, as most Christian married couples have, are you walking contrary to the Bible's mentality and limiting what God desires for you?

I'll answer that question with an illustration from our journey. People often ask Veronica and me, "How many kids do you want?" Interestingly, we don't want a plan for children. For us, kids aren't some mathematical equation or a five-year outline. This question also implies that *we* are somehow the author of our families. Far too many of us are convinced that we are the ones who bring our families into existence. We are the ones who are the producers of life. But this is a mistaken way to think, for a Christian it is out of step with how the Word of God attributes the authorship of children.

In 2015 Veronica and I decided to yield our hearts to this biblical perspective. To submit our plan and preference regarding the number of kids God might desire to give us. That could be three or it could be ten, and we will always consider health risks and reality. As a husband, 1 Peter 3:7 instructs me to "dwell with [my wife] according to knowledge, giving honour unto the wife, as unto the weaker vessel, and as being heirs together of the grace of life; that your prayers be not hindered" (KJV).

For Veronica and I, our hearts are surrendered. Like most of you, we love children and would never want to

Do you want more of God's blessings?

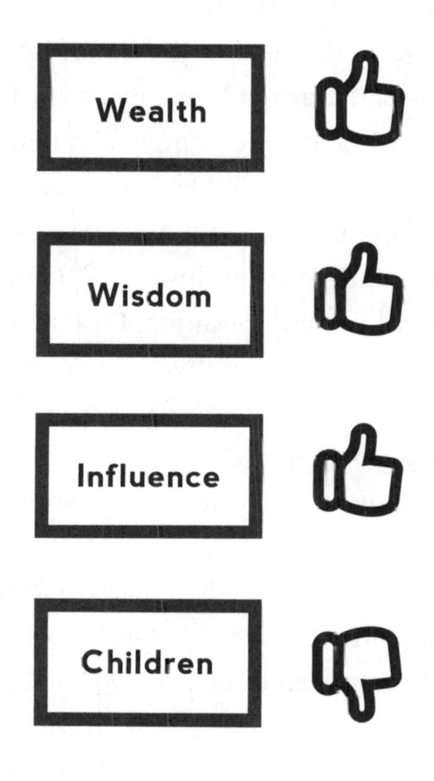

prevent such an incredible blessing from entering our lives. What about you? Are you open to surrendering the number of children you want to have and allowing God to author your family? Because God is not interested in the diminishing of His people on the planet. His foundational instruction to Adam, "Be fruitful and multiply,"[5] is said again to Noah. By this critical restatement, we know God is not simply commanding us to, "Create more bodies!" Why? He just wiped out millions of bodies in the Great Flood. No, His command is to "create more children who love Me!" God isn't interested in unfruitful multiplication. He's interested in the creation and raising of children who know Him, obey Him, and love Him.

So let's reverse engineer the conversation. If you're a Christian, I'd like to ask you a few questions.

- Do you believe children are a blessing (Psalm 127:3–5; Matthew 18:1–6; Mark 9:37; 10:14)?
- What about their existence? Do you believe God is the Author of life (Genesis 4:25; 17:6, 16; 20:17–18; 26:4; 30:2; 33:5; Leviticus 26:9, 22; Deuteronomy 7:13; 10:22; 30:5, 9; 1 Samuel 2:21; Psalm 107:41; 127:3; 139:13–16; Isaiah 29:23; Jeremiah 1:5; 30:19)?

- How about control? Do you believe God will give you only what you can handle (Romans 8:38–39; 1 Corinthians 1:8; 10:13; Philippians 1:6; 1 John 5:4)?
- Do you desire to relinquish the authority of your life to God? In other words, do you want His will to be done in your life (Psalm 143:10; Proverbs 3:5–6; Matthew 6:10; Luke 9:23; 22:42; Hebrews 13:20–21)?

Many of you answered yes to each of those questions. However, selecting the correct answer on a multiple-choice exam and choosing to own the consequences of those biblical beliefs are two different things. This is a common gap found in today's churches.

In my experience the average Christian couple responds to God more like, "Your will be done . . . in every area except this one." So I ask you to reflect on this: If we, as Christians, believe these things to be true, can we have a child outside of God's will for us? I'm certain the millions of couples fighting through infertility would say absolutely not. So, if it's true that we cannot have a child outside of God's will for us, is it also true that we can only have the children God intended us to have? Now, I'm not claiming ultimate authority on this matter, nor am I prepared to dive into the wide theological debate on this topic. These are deep heart matters.

"Be fruitful and multiply," does not simply mean, "Create more bodies!" No, His command is to "create more children who love Me!"

—DALE PARTRIDGE

What I'm illuminating here is simply a perspective of Scripture I'm calling us to examine. I'm not saying that all people must be parents. I'm not attempting to shame your vasectomy or birth-control habits. I am merely asking Christian couples who have answered yes to my questions, and yet have chosen not to yield their hearts in the matter of children, to prayerfully consider these ideas.

Interestingly, on our wedding day we didn't know if we even wanted children. Sadly, we viewed kids as a restraint to our success. But similar to how you are being challenged to evaluate the Bible's perspective on children, Veronica and I had a parallel experience with an older couple. Essentially, they softly and patiently helped us realize that every reason we used to justify our stance against children wasn't based in healthy biblical thinking but fell into one of three unbiblical categories: selfishness, faithlessness, or fear.

I remember the night when, instead of telling Veronica and I how we should view children, they asked us to go home, sit in front of a whiteboard, and draw out three vertical columns. Next, they instructed us to title each column with one of three words: selfishness, faithlessness, and fear. Next, they urged us to list out each of the reasons we had chosen to prevent children and decide if any of them fit within these categories. I'm sure you can predict how this story ends. Every reason we had found itself in a column. It was an eye-opening experiencing to say the least.

At the time, we had already had our first baby (Aria), and she changed everything. She brought joy, love, and maturity to our lives. Then, just months after our whiteboard experience Harbor (a miscarriage) challenged our new-found faith in God's doctrine on children. But shortly after came Honor (our second born), who affirmed our decision to let God author our family, with his soft spirit and love for his big sister. But today we're officially outnumbered with our third born, Valor! And I can tell you that the blessings have multiplied with each child.

One direct example from our life is how our children have forced Veronica and I to grow up, know up, and show up. In other words, they have pushed us to put on our grown-up pants and become responsible, biblical adults. It's counterintuitive but true: we must raise someone younger in order to properly grow older.

And the blessing of children is not just for you; your children will also bless the world. They will carry on your legacy of godliness long after you're gone. I once heard a story about a woman who found out she was

The Anti-Justification Station

Selfishness	Faithlessness	Fear
✓	✓	✓
✓		✓

CULTURE SAYS:

~~Children will impede your dreams.~~

WHAT GOD HAS TAUGHT ME:

Children should be the dream.

pregnant and had already born seven children. Three were deaf, two were blind, and one was mentally handicapped. In addition, she was afflicted with syphilis. Would you recommend she have an abortion? Would you say she had too many children already? If so, you just killed the most iconic pianist in history: Beethoven. The point is, by attempting to control God's design for our family, we don't know what lives we're preventing. How many world changers, leaders, musicians, and heroes have been put to death before they were even born? As Pastor Andy Stanley says, "Your greatest contribution to the kingdom of God may not be something you do but someone you raise."[6]

If you want to be successful, don't fear children. Fear an empty home in your twilight years. Fear your own selfishness. Fear your own fear.

03

Money

It's called *hedonic adaptation*, and you've experienced it even if you've never heard of it. Researchers use this phrase to refer to the tendency of humans to return to a normal level of happiness after gaining material wealth or goods. You purchase a luxury car, and your endorphins rise. You wash it and buff it and sit in it and show it off and feel a high for weeks or even months. But soon you take it for granted, and it just becomes another *thing* in your pile of *stuff*. Now you're no happier than you were before you purchased the car. But you have a massive monthly car payment, and you realize that materialism promises more than it delivers. That's hedonic adaptation.

Interestingly, some scientists refer to this phenomenon as the *hedonic treadmill*. I like this name better because it explains what success, materialism, and money do to us. It lures us into physical motion but takes us nowhere. Sweat falls, but we go nowhere. Breathing quickens, but we go nowhere. Calories burn, but we're exactly where we started. The rat race turns out to be a hamster wheel, which is also the deeper meaning behind this book's cover imagery.

The cultural definition of success always involves money, even if we're not brave enough to admit it. If you're working at a job earning minimum wage, it doesn't matter if you're happy or living your calling; you'll be hard-pressed to find someone who'll call you "successful." Meanwhile, you could be the most miserable jerk with two legs and a mouth, but if you're swimming in a pool of gold coins, you'll find yourself envied among your peers.

Sadly, this particular cultural perspective has been adopted by not a few Christians. In churches that teach the prosperity gospel, pastors flaunt their wealth and fly around on private jets. They preach sermons about God wanting us to have the best and shun the rest. People in these church communities work themselves to death in pursuit of money because they believe that's what God wants for them; however, when they attain the wealth they so desperately sought they soon recognize how bankrupt they still remain.

The Bible is alarmingly cautious about money. It isn't even neutral. It claims that money is deceptive, and the pursuit of it is like running on a treadmill. The psalmist warned, "If riches increase, do not set your heart on them."[1] Ecclesiastes 5:10 says, "He who loves silver will not be satisfied with silver; nor he who loves abundance, with increase. This also is vanity." Jesus said that "the cares of this world, the deceitfulness of riches, and the desires for other things entering in choke the word, and it becomes unfruitful."[2] He described the Pharisees as "lovers of money."[3]

One of my favorite verses about money comes from the apostle Paul in 1 Timothy 6:7–10:

> For we brought nothing into this world, and it is certain we can carry nothing out. And having food and clothing, with these we shall be content. But those who desire to be rich fall into temptation and a snare, and into many foolish and harmful lusts which drown men in destruction and perdition. For the love of money is a root of all kinds of evil, for which some have strayed from the faith in their greediness, and pierced themselves through with many sorrows. (NKJV)

The Bible urges us to be cautious of wealth and content with what we have. Can you imagine how different the world would be if this were true of us all? There would be no shoplifting. No one would lie about their co-worker to steal a promotion. People wouldn't traumatically uproot their families and move halfway across the country for a 10 percent raise. And churches and charities wouldn't have to beg for donations.

If we all adopted the Bible's perspective, America also wouldn't be languishing in our current debt crisis. The average household has $16,000 in credit card balances and a total debt just shy of $132,500.[4] Our churches aren't much better, often taking out massive lines of credit to build giant buildings with fancy accoutrements and six-digit landscaping budgets. And our government might be the worst of all, amassing a debt with an embarrassing number of zeros and a century of work required to remove it.

When Veronica and I first got married, she came in with pristine finances. She was totally organized, had never borrowed any money, and had even put some cash away in her savings account. But unfortunately for her, she married a total financial nightmare. I came into the marriage with nearly $80,000 in debt. And this was not student loans or something at least seemingly admirable. It was from cars I couldn't afford, credit card balances with crippling interest rates, and even small

CULTURE SAYS:

~~If you've got lots of money, relax; you're standing on thick ice.~~

WHAT GOD HAS TAUGHT ME:

If you've got lots of money, be watchful; you're standing on thin ice.

purchases like name-brand groceries and new computers when my old ones still worked. I even had a hefty IRS tax bill for which I was on a payment plan and doling out crazy fees. All things considered, I was paying about $2,000 per month in minimum debt payments, which was a sizeable portion of our income.

The funny thing is we never acknowledged that this was a problem, which is where most couples really go astray. There was a giant elephant in the room, and we were just vacuuming around him.

I'll share another example. We live on a farm, which means I have to go out at night and feed our animals. When I head outside, I take a 700 lumen LED flashlight along to guide me to the cow paddock, wood shed, or chicken coop. Every once in a while I'll become fearful to shine my flashlight too far into the distance. Since we're surrounded by hundreds of acres of trees, we have an active population of wildlife. There could be a pack of coyotes out there. Or a mountain lion. Or a herd of elk. So in my nervousness, I keep the light away from the darkness. In other words, my fear of being aware wasn't making me any safer; it actually made me more vulnerable. Interestingly, we do this in life too—refusing to shine a light on our darkness for fear of what we'll find out.

In 2012 we met a couple at the church we attended who encouraged us to shine the light directly at our darkness. And they weren't older than we were. They were peers. Equally as "successful" as we were. But with one exception: they were debt-free. I discussed finances with the husband, and he talked about debt from a biblical position: as a curse. As something to be avoided at all costs. The longer I spoke to him, the more embarrassed I was and the more I realized how irresponsible I had been. After this conversation, Veronica and I decided not to just shine our light but to keep our light on our spending habits and personal finances. We put together a painful budget and decided to get out of debt. We decided, as Dave Ramsey says, "to punch debt in the face until its nose bleeds."

The problem is that the only way to get out of debt is making more money and spending less. So I had to work even harder and we had to cut back our expenses to the bones. We sold everything that we absolutely didn't need and even asked friends for anything they would allow us to sell online for a profit. It took years of hard work, but today I am proud to say that we are debt-free. We do not have any credit cards or car payments, and we don't buy anything unless we can afford it. We put 65 percent down on the house we have recently paid off and just purchased our third rental property.

During our debt desert, I learned three money lessons that helped us create the financial maturity we needed and the lifestyle we could be proud of:

1. Money made quickly is often money lost quickly. The journey to healthy wealth was painful for us. We cut, slashed, unlearned, and relearned. However, I can't imagine Veronica and myself being capable of responsibly managing our level of income now without it. It reminds me of Jesus' famous words in the parable of the talents: "You were faithful over a few things, I will make you ruler over many things."[5] Too often we want to divorce qualification from training. We want the maturity without the growth. Sadly, I've seen more people lose money they weren't qualified to steward than I can count. Instead, be patient on your journey to generating wealth. Every struggle has its purpose. Your income journey is not an exception.
2. If you want something you've never had, you must do something you've never done. Most people's dreams are bigger than their nine-to-five

paychecks. Which means if you have big vision, strong calling, or a desire to make huge change, your job by itself likely won't fund it. Something *must* change. For us, it meant self-employment. For you, it might simply require adding an income stream, launching an online store, or making an investment. Either way, big change demands two things: time and money. If you're stuck under a financial ceiling and chained to an emotionless forty-hour work week, you might be clipping your own wings. Escaping the prison of the professional employee isn't easy. Make a plan and attack it. And chip away at the concrete that holds you in. You only get one life. Don't spend it inside the walls of a job that's holding you back.

3. **If you can't pay cash, you can't afford it.** Dave Ramsey often says, "Act your wage!" The culture's mentality of false need is merely a lack of discipline, a delusion, and a sense of entitlement. My good friend Dr. John Townsend said, "You have to learn the difference between a need, which should be met, and an entitled desire, which should be starved."[6] We must get to a point in our spiritual maturity where we start a budget, tell our money where to go, and stop buying

"You have to learn the difference between a need, which should be met, and an entitled desire, which should be starved."

—DR. JOHN TOWNSEND

> things we can't afford. Ultimately, we have to tell ourselves no so later we can tell ourselves yes.

It took me making millions to realize money would never make me happy. And it took me drowning in debt to realize how horrible debt is. Veronica and I did exactly the opposite of what the Bible teaches. We took on the curse (debt), and because of that we put off the blessing (children). Debt is a common cause of the reduction of family, freedom, and fun.

The world will try to tell you that you *need* stuff to be successful. But don't listen to them. It's a lie that will land you in a life you never wanted. It will put you on a treadmill that will promise you progress but take you nowhere.

Purpose

Why do you do what you do? It's a simple question, but one that many people never ask themselves. Most people find themselves in accidental careers and, when meeting new people, begin to naively drop tragic statements like, "I never intended to be in the [enter almost any noun] industry, but here I am."

When I entered the great American workforce at seventeen, my career choices were purely reactionary. I needed to pay bills, so I'd pick up a new project. A friend said I should launch something, so I did. I noticed a need in the marketplace, so I filled it. My early career choices were driven strictly by insecurity and worry and necessity. And that's not all bad. You don't always get to do what you love when you're young. Sometimes you have to force yourself to love what you do.

But unchecked, reactionary career drifting almost always ends up as a life sentence of mediocrity, monotony, and dissatisfaction. Most people wake up thirty years later in a job they don't love, chained to a desk they despise, secretly wondering how they got there but publicly pretending like they planned it. But life has taught me this: we get the results we planned for. That being said, the majority of people either don't have a plan, have a bad plan, or—out of a lack of discipline—they stray from their plan.

So how do you make a change? For some reason, many of us have chosen to compartmentalize our careers from our Creator. Colossians 3:17 says, "And whatever you do in word or deed, do all in the name of the Lord Jesus." Proverbs 16:3 continues with, "Commit your works to the LORD, and your thoughts will be established." Sadly, most people want a calling without considering who is doing the actual "calling." Instead, people seem to be over-called, by turning every new opportunity into "their calling," or falsely called, by camouflaging what "makes them happy" or what "their heart desires" as work that God has divinely laid upon their life. Give me a break. The Bible teaches a different idea. An idea that each of us has been called to something, and our job is to seek it, find it, and be faithful to it.

In the Old Testament Abraham was called to launch a nation, Moses was called to lead that nation, David was called to rule over that nation, and Isaiah was called to speak truth to that nation. In the New Testament Mary was called to birth a man who would become a Savior, and Jesus was called to be the man who would save the world. Then there were the apostles, followed by those who canonized the Bible, only to be succeeded by the saints—Francis of Assisi and Luther and Tyndale and Wesley and Wilberforce. Finally, there were those who are a part of our modern timeline, from C. S. Lewis and Mother Teresa to Martin Luther King Jr. and Billy Graham. Each person had a divine calling, a divine purpose. As Christians we cannot trivialize the work God has for us. We cannot vandalize it into mere passion or excitement or desire. Calling is much more than work to be done; it is work that must be done.

It's my belief that God has implanted in every person a purpose which they are uniquely appointed to accomplish. Something with divine significance and meaning. Ultimately, work that stems from your natural giftings, aspirations, and story. Work that brings order into chaos and injects God's DNA into the world. This calling can be pursued in a range of occupations, but it should be pursued. Sadly, many fail to find it. Their illiteracy of the Bible, the book that they claim has authority in their lives, and their unwillingness to fanatically seek the will of their Father prevent them from the spiritual maturity required to know one's life work.

Two quotes have assisted me in unearthing the work I was made to do: "Just because you can doesn't mean you should" and "Just because it's smart doesn't mean it's right." But saying no to opportunities, especially smart ones when they are within arm's reach, is downright difficult. Developing the restraint to question and evaluate if every move is bringing you closer to God's calling for you or distracting you from it is laborious. Ultimately, we must be mature enough not to let what we want to do prevent us from what we're meant to do.

In 2010 I launched a faith-based entrepreneurship company with a flagship event titled the Identity Conference. I saw an opportunity to provide content for Christians in business who wanted to bridge the gap between faith and the workplace. We hosted our first event in Southern California at a megachurch, and one thousand people showed up to hear speakers like *New York Times* bestselling author Dr. John Townsend and "America's Pastor" Rick Warren. The energy was high,

Obsession with Reading The Bible

Fanatical Prayer Life

Rapid Spiritual Maturation

Calling Revealed

and I made an honest income doing it, but by its third year I shut it down.

While this might seem like work at the center of my wheelhouse, it was merely a remnant of my reactionary nature from my late teens and early twenties. I knew I could make money doing it, but that wasn't the same as being called. I knew there was a need for it, but that wasn't the same as being called. I thought it was fun, but that wasn't the same as being called. I worked overtime to pretend that I was called to it, but in my heart I was putting lipstick on a pig. I couldn't sustain that facade any longer.

This experience taught me that purpose is when you're both equally gifted and qualified for the role that is in front of you. As for the Identity Conference, I had the gifting to make it work; however, I wasn't qualified to shepherd a conference for business leaders far more mature than I was. I didn't have the depth of experience, much less the wisdom to share, at twenty-five years old. If you're gifted at something but not qualified, then you'll eventually be exposed. If you're qualified but not gifted, you'll be respected but not effective. You need both.

I think of King David, who became king in his thirties, not at seventeen. This wasn't a coincidence. He was

If you're gifted at something but not qualified, then you'll eventually be exposed. If you're qualified but not gifted, you'll be respected but not effective. You need both.

—DALE PARTRIDGE

anointed early and was a gifted young man, but as we see in the book of 1 Samuel, he wasn't qualified until he was much older. God required a season of growth between His "yes" and His "go." A season learning the lessons of humility, self-control, and obedience. You see, most Christians turn God's "yes" into God's "go," an almost similar debacle of turning our giftedness into qualification. As a result, we find ourselves out of step with God's will, unprepared for the work in front us, and overwhelmed with the work we thought we would love.

Going back to the illustration in 1 Samuel, we see David's patience as he spent years running from Saul, refusing to take the throne by might. He even had opportunities to kill Saul but didn't. He waited for his qualifications to catch up to his gifting. He waited for God's "go" to be clear as day. Being king was the right thing for him, but he had to wait for the right time.

You see, most of us are more concerned with the work God has for us and less worried about His timing. We pridefully rush into the colosseum far before we're ready. But the Bible has taught me a sobering truth about what God's call on our lives means. It's taught me that while God does have big plans for His obedient children, He has far more work to do in us than through us.

God has far more work to do in us than through us. Meaning while *we're* looking out, toward our destiny, He's looking in at our maturity.

—DALE PARTRIDGE

Meaning while *we're* looking out, toward our destiny, He's looking in at our maturity.

I believe the most dangerous people on the planet are those with a gifting that outweighs their state of maturity. That's why we have bankrupt athletes, multi-divorced actors and actresses, overdosing musicians, law-breaking celebrities, and dishonest politicians.

As both leaders and Christians, we must learn to separate a person's gifting from their maturity (or immaturity). Fame doesn't equal maturity. Athletic ability doesn't equal maturity. An amazing sermon doesn't equal maturity. Again, these are gifts—many of which are recognized as early as childhood. But as Christians looking to live within God's will, we must learn not only to develop our gifting but to embrace the timing that's required to mature us for the work we're meant to do. Remember, your intrinsic gifts will not go away, but neither will the public's memory of you stepping into a position of power before you were ready.

While you're discerning your purpose and waiting for the right moment, you're forced to live in the in-between time. As you pursue your calling with patience, you'll encounter many assignments in many seasons. Be faithful in those assignments, but don't confuse them for your ultimate purpose. As author Brad Lomenick

CULTURE SAYS:

~~Follow your heart and pursue what makes you happy.~~

WHAT GOD HAS TAUGHT ME:

Your heart wasn't designed to be followed but to be led by My Holy Spirit.

wrote in *H3 Leadership*, "There is a marked difference between a calling and an assignment, and failing to recognize it is a one-way ticket to the frustration station."[1]

One of the biggest lies of the culture is that following your heart is the wisest thing you can do for yourself. The Bible says the heart is deceitful. It cannot be trusted. Rather than follow your heart, the wisest thing you can do is guide your heart. That's how you were created. Your heart was not designed to be followed. It was designed to be led—by God's Word, the Holy Spirit, and your brothers and sisters in Christ.

But all of this leaves a big question unanswered: What is *your* purpose? Unfortunately, I can't tell you that. Your purpose is a treasure that only you can unearth through prayer, discernment, and wise counsel.

But I can help you rule out many possible diversions: your calling must complement rather than compete with your values. If pursuing something places insupportable pressure on your family or strains your marriage, that is not your calling. If chasing something would diminish your dignity or the dignity of others, that is not your calling. If embracing something would require feeding your sense of ego or greed, that is not your calling. You may be tempted to believe that your values and calling are flexible, but God's call never

Your heart was not designed to be followed. It was designed to be led—by God's Word, the Holy Spirit, and your brothers and sisters in Christ.

—DALE PARTRIDGE

compromises His Word. Calling must flow from your beliefs and convictions and priorities, rather than push against them.

I believe 1 Corinthians 10:31 sums up *purpose* nicely: "Therefore, whether you eat or drink, or whatever you do, do all to the glory of God." This verse explains both the constraints and freedoms of purpose. It reduces its point to activities as simple as eating and drinking but extends its territory out to "whatever you do," making it clear that all of our actions are to glorify God. This scripture offers us unlimited expressions in our choice for career, job, passion, or profession. Sure, those choices must not include the practicing of sin, but we have freedom to express our righteous desires as long as God receives the glory.

Influence

A few years ago, I was called out for tweeting uncited quotations. It was never my intention to mislead people, but it was ultimately my fault. I had asked my assistant to comb through Pinterest, Tumblr, and Google to find a thousand quotes, adding them to an automated social media queue on Twitter. Many of these were anonymous or unclear sources of general wisdom, but others had a clear author and were not cited. Out of laziness and living at too fast a pace, I never went back to track down the appropriate citations. As a result, it appeared other people's words originated with me, as if their wisdom were mine.

The gentleman who called me out was relentless, and my first impulse was to be defensive and ignore the situation. After all, why should I care what some guy on the Internet thinks about me? But it soon hit me: *I need to stop this.* This wasn't a time for pride; this was a time for humility. It didn't matter if anyone else participated in or accepted similar practices; I shouldn't emulate the dishonest behaviors of others. I stopped the automation, wrote the man an apology, and penned a blog post publicly taking the blame for what had happened.

I did this for two reasons. First, through the Holy Spirit I became convicted that what I did was unwise and needed to be corrected. And second, my reputation was on the line. Defensiveness was not the solution. Pride was not the solution. As Christians, we're expected to live exemplary lives. Above reproach. A cultural example. Consequently, we don't get to act like other people. We have a stricter code of ethics to follow. And we should be humble enough to admit when we fail.

King Solomon once said, "A good name is to be chosen rather than great riches."[1] What others say about you is more important than what you say about yourself. In other words, I needed to spend more time thinking about a better name than my bottom line. You can't have a good name if you have a past of hurting others. You can't have a good name if you refuse to apologize. You can't have a good name if you care more about being right than making things right.

This is the opposite of what the world will often tell you. The culture says, "It doesn't matter what other people think about you. Just be true to yourself." But the Bible teaches that the path to influence is fueled by reputation. Worry about your reputation, and let God take care of the rest.

Having a sound reputation might be the most important indicator of authentic, long-term success. For most of us, it takes years to construct a reliable name in our industry, and as Warren Buffet once said, "It takes 20 years to build a reputation and five minutes to lose it. If you think about that, you'll do things differently." This doesn't mean that we should live in the fear of men. Or become people-pleasers. Or judge our every move on the wind of public opinion. But if even one respectable and faithful person thinks poorly of you, you'd be wise to reconsider your ways.

Recently, I was scheduled to interview a photographer who is massively famous on Instagram. Leading up to the interview, I had several friends call, e-mail, and warn me about how they had seriously negative experiences with him. One even told me that he was a "jerk." I typically give people the benefit of the doubt when I hear things like this, so I decided to go ahead with the podcast interview.

A few minutes into our conversation, I knew I was in trouble. Despite my clear instructions of locating an inactive environment, he called me from a noisy room, and when I asked if he could move somewhere quieter, he declined. He sounded distracted with every response, as though he was working on something else while he was talking to me. Then a few minutes into the interview, I heard him get up and walk down the hall. A door swung open.

And . . .

Then . . .

The sound of him urinating into the toilet was clearly audible on the audio. I looked at my podcast producer, and we were both slack-jawed. I quickly wrapped up the interview and never aired it. His reputation preceded him, and he lived up to it. He was famous among his fans and infamous among his peers.

My guest on the podcast that day was like a lot of people. In their pursuit of fame, they have done the easy work of self-promotion while ignoring the difficult work of character development. Christians, pay attention to this mistake and don't duplicate it in your life. Refuse to become the most influential person that nobody likes.

CULTURE SAYS:

~~Become a person of influence by achieving great fame.~~

WHAT GOD HAS TAUGHT ME:

Become a person of character by attaining a good reputation.

A bad reputation has a ruthless way of catching up to you. And it doesn't matter if you have a great family, if you are in good health, or if you are flush with cash and even have great friends knocking down your door; if you have a poor reputation, eventually everything will crumble.

But what happens when what God calls good, culture calls bad? What if living well is viewed as living wrong? As you probably have noticed, we live in a time when the Bible's teachings of good character are considered offensive, bigoted, and even close-minded.

But this shouldn't be a surprise. Jesus warned us about these times in Matthew 10:21–28:

> Now brother will deliver up brother to death, and a father his child; and children will rise up against parents and cause them to be put to death. And you will be hated by all for My name's sake. But he who endures to the end will be saved. When they persecute you in this city, flee to another. . . .
>
> A disciple is not above his teacher, nor a servant above his master. It is enough for a disciple that he be like his teacher, and a servant like his master. If they have called the master of the house Beelzebub [a demon], how much more will they call those of

> his household! Therefore do not fear them. For there is nothing covered that will not be revealed, and hidden that will not be known.
>
> Whatever I tell you in the dark, speak in the light; and what you hear in the ear, preach on the housetops. And do not fear those who kill the body but cannot kill the soul. But rather fear Him who is able to destroy both soul and body in hell.

Jesus was saying that maintaining a good reputation with Him will cost you. A cost so high that the offense to others will even surpass natural affection between siblings and parents. A cost so high that honoring what Jesus honors will cause people to persecute you, hate you, and possibly even kill you. A telling perspective for today's megachurch pastors who are seemingly avoiding such persecution while gaining popularity in the public square. Nevertheless, Jesus' instruction is not to be quiet. His instruction is to be wise, to speak the full truth, to live loud, to love people to the point of confusion, and to not fear the world's perception of your godly character.

A bad reputation with the world will cost your popularity. A bad reputation with God will cost your eternity. The Lord wants us to aim for respect and

A bad reputation with the
world will cost your popularity.
A bad reputation with God
will cost your eternity.

—DALE PARTRIDGE

integrity in every relationship. However, He never wants us to compromise His Word in the process. Reputation for the Christian is a balancing act of faith. We must be in the world but not of it. We must honor others but not more than we honor Him.

So, how do you achieve fame?

By promoting yourself, pleasing others, and increasing your influence.

How do you achieve a good reputation?

By humbling yourself, pleasing God, and developing good character.

The choice is yours.

Freedom

Once you have children, striking up random conversations with other parents becomes a common occurrence. And sometimes these conversations become fertile soil for a budding friendship. I met James at the Old Mill District in Bend while our kids were playing next to the river. He had been a highly successful entrepreneur by our culture's standards and understood what being in the public eye was like. Veronica also really connected with his wife, which is significant because she is more of an introvert than I am. It's exceptional when we get along with other couples equally.

We found ourselves lost in conversation with James and his wife that day and exchanged numbers as we left. On our way home, Veronica and I talked about how excited we were to have found new friends with kids of similar age. But the relationship after that day was not nearly as effortless.

I texted James a few days later to see if they wanted to meet us in town for drinks that weekend, but he said they were busy. The next week would be better, he informed me. But when I called to invite them to dinner at our home the following week, he said that one of their children was sick. The very next day James said they would be having dinner as a family an hour from our home (their child apparently felt better), and we could join them if we wanted. We dropped everything and met them. Driving home, Veronica and I felt encouraged again.

The next week the relationship seemed to devolve once more. We kept asking to spend time with them, and they always seemed to have a reason why they couldn't. But every time they asked us to come to them, Veronica and I were there.

Now, all of their excuses were valid in one-off experiences. But when the occasional excuse became the pattern of the relationship, they were simply revealing the priority of their hearts: independence and a friendship that operated on their terms.

I'm going to go out on a limb here and guess that

most people reading these words have experienced a relationship like this before. Or perhaps you are the one on the other side of the story, always finding an excuse while expecting others to be there for you. Actually, most people today are like James and his wife. They are living their own lives, making space for others only when it is convenient for them.

This way of engaging relationships is not actually the problem. Seriously, it's not. No, this way of engaging relationships is a symptom of the actual problem. We live in a society that has come to worship individual or family freedom. It values autonomy above all else. It strives for individualism and independence over commitment and sacrifice.

For many, the religion of freedom is founded in the doctrine of open-mindedness. Being open-minded is our culture's way to creatively remove the need for a moral code. The world has even packaged this idea as "intellectual" or "progressive," making it a convenient ploy for those with no conviction or submission to unchanging values or to a relationship with God.

As Christians, we must ask ourselves: What are the immovable boundaries we subscribe to? Because if everything is subject to complete-freedom theology, then nothing is truly right and truly wrong. Now, I do believe there are plenty of areas we, as believers, must remain "open" to; however, there are many areas to which we must remain closed-minded. Areas that are not freedoms but prisons, snares, and confinements to our hopes for true success.

To make hard harder, this cultural motif is central to the world's definition of success. Our culture urges us to work as hard as we can to become as free as we can to be as successful as we can. Climbing the corporate ladder is equal to success because it allows you to dictate your own calendar. Being the boss is equal to success because you don't have to submit to hierarchy. Owning your own business is success because you get to call all the shots. Making lots of money is success because you can buy whatever you desire and travel to your dream destinations. Why would you give up the freedom you've worked so hard to achieve? Why would you choose submission, commitment, yielding, consideration, and giving preference to others?

But the Bible calls us to a different way of living. As Solomon said, "A man who isolates himself seeks his own desire; he rages against all wise judgment."[1] God has neither instructed us nor designed us for "convenient" community. Nowhere does His Word promote us as autonomous beings fulfilling our calling in seclusion.

In other words, unity, oneness, commitment to one another, and the illustration of "one body" is our absolute directive.

Consider what the author of Hebrews wrote in chapter 10 verses 24–25: "And let us consider one another in order to stir up love and good works, not forsaking the assembling of ourselves together, as is the manner of some, but exhorting one another, and so much the more as you see the Day approaching." Many Christians live in a place of spiritual frustration, each one wondering why their walk with God and His church doesn't align with the narrative and testimonies they read in the Bible. Sadly, they are causing their own dissatisfaction because they are avoiding the closeness required to "bear one another's burdens"[2] and the commitment needed to "confess your trespasses to one another, and pray for one another, that you may be healed."[3] The vast majority of our churches are not fostering these types of connections.

You see, while our culture seeks the freedom to have sex with whomever we want, spend our money however we want, and live and travel whenever and wherever we want, we ultimately experience the results we *didn't* want—results of constantly seeking our own desires. Results of an unforeseen bondage to self-centeredness that leaves us lonely, unable to produce committed relationships, and content with a human experience inferior to what we're designed for.

Christians, however, are powerful when joined with others in biblical community. Not only do we reap the deep waters of affection and devotion, but we are less inclined to morally fall when we are willing to commit, to know, and to be known. In turn, our lives are a threat to the work of our Enemy, and we are protected through wisdom, counsel, and our willingness to be surrounded by friends who offer correction and loving rebuke.

Essentially, ultimate freedom isn't playing it safe or smart. We live in a culture that has trained people to believe their availability has no impact on the state of their relational health. What a lie.

It is stillness and availability and accessibility that are the true currencies of relationship success. It is othering and preference and willingness that lead to emotional wealth.

This may sound radical to you. After all, even most American Christian churches don't teach or promote this way of being. Grievously, most churches are not biblical. They are designed to prevent this very concept. We see this through their event-based model, where audience members join as inactive spectators of

Christians are powerful when joined with others in biblical community.

—DALE PARTRIDGE

a weekly monologue—and because we are designed for depth rather than breadth, many people who "attend" church end up falling away.

Ultimately, cool worship music begins to wear thin when their souls find that they are surrounded by people but are in relationship with no one. They head toward the revolving door in the back because they didn't find what the Bible promised. They never felt what Jesus said about His people and His church. And unfortunately, most pastors have chosen to look away from this doctrinal way of living because it doesn't scale easily. Particularly, closeness doesn't pay the bills. So instead, they rig an injection of this Christian necessity into "small groups" and hope it leaves their sheep with enough nourishment to keep them giving on Sunday.

So why the big struggle? Community is made up of a couple components. Two are highly unpopular. The first is honesty. Think about the three closest people to you. How far are you willing to let them in? Do they know the state of your marriage, the condition of your obedience to God's commands, and the darkest struggles of your life? As I mentioned earlier, the Bible instructs us to "bear one another's burdens." It doesn't support culture's "come this far but no farther" approach to intimacy. So if you don't have honesty, you don't have community.

Cultural Worship

Freedom
Autonomy
Independence
Individualism

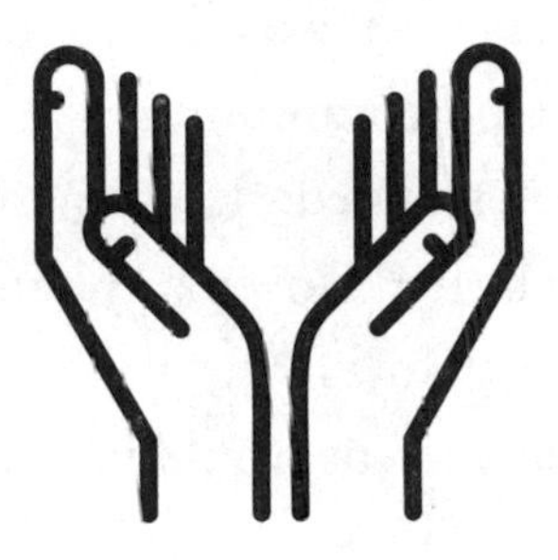

The second component is accountability. Because the Bible instructs us to "confess your trespasses to one another, and pray for one another, that you may be healed," we must be willing to confront or be confronted by one another when we exhibit unhealthy patterns. Furthermore, we must be inclined to submit ourselves to the authority of not just our leaders but our peers. You see, our community's prayer life is directly connected to our shared life. We can only pray for and bear together the burdens we know about. Independence isn't the path to freedom but to captivity. Autonomy isn't the way to painlessness but to quiet suffering. If you don't have accountability, you don't have community.

How many divorces would have been prevented if people were in true community? How many suicides would have been stopped? How many cries for help would have been heard? How many bankruptcies would have been avoided? How many affairs would have been evaded? How many needs would have been met?

Now, there's nothing more stressful than trying to solve a problem that has no solution. So where do you go from here? How can you find biblical community? How can you begin pursuing a life of real Christian relationships?

You have two options: you either plant it or find it.

CULTURE SAYS:

~~You should fight to achieve freedom and autonomy.~~

WHAT GOD HAS TAUGHT ME:

You should fight to find a biblical community with fanatical accountability.

You either seek God's navigation for your life and ask Him to reveal the remnants of counter-cultural, biblical communities that are scattered across the world, or you create it. Now as many of you know, it's just about impossible to create something you've never experienced. That's why Veronica and I have chosen to devote the rest of our lives to helping people find this. If you're interested in learning more, consider our nonprofit program at UnlearnChurch.org.

In the end, you can have real relationships or you can have personal freedom. But you can't have both. Think about it. When you're young, you establish a relationship with your parents, which requires relinquishing your freedom. When you get married, your commitment requires relinquishing your freedom. When you give your life to Jesus, your salvation requires relinquishing your freedom. This is the way relationship works. This is the way community works.

Veronica and I have submitted our freedom to the biblical church community that meets in the homes of our members. We wouldn't buy a house without consulting these people first. We wouldn't consider a career change without talking to them in depth. We wouldn't move to another place without asking their blessing. We're not living alone. We're living alongside these people. Which means I don't get to make life changes without considering them. I don't get to sin without considering them. I don't get to win without considering them. I don't even get to publish this manuscript without considering them. But while my freedom is lower, my sense of fulfillment and safety is higher than it has ever been.

True success means finding the courage to enter into a relationship on another person's terms. It means refusing to be an entity unto yourself. It means being willing to have tough conversations and answer tough questions. It means making lifelong commitments to a spouse and to a faith and to a community. It means being dependent on God and dependent on mature believers who love you.

Wisdom says that the fastest path to maturity is within the hardest relationships we have. You can certainly avoid all of these duties; just know that you're also avoiding the ultimate development—of you.

07

Youth

We are the first culture in history where the elderly are despised and the youth are worshipped.

Stanford University professor Robert Harrison studied literature, history, and philosophy and concluded that we have become the "youngest" society on earth. What does this mean? "The young have become a model of emulation for the older population, rather than the other way around," he said.[1]

If you don't think this is true, just visit your local shopping mall. You'll see moms dressed like daughters and fathers dressed like sons. Adults use the language of teenagers, not realizing how awkward they sound. And instead of disciplining their children, parents opt for the position of friend.

Look at the gyms and fitness centers. A place filled with people hiding their fear of time in an adult playground filled with eye candy, narcissism, and shallow goals. How have we arrived at this place? How have we transitioned to the glorification of youth and the resistance of age?

Our perverted definition of beauty and our obsession with it have certainly played a role. We worship vanity and a fleshly desire to appear twenty when we are forty. But why does our culture think that's better? Why would a society prefer such a thing? In part, it is a reaction. With the intelligence gap caused by the Internet age, older people are now seen as irrelevant. As a result, culture has incentivized looking young simply to fulfill the need to be seen and heard and employed.

Going deeper, it is also a response from a faithless culture struggling to have hope after death—and instead of accepting reality and looking to the fruits of age and the afterlife, we desperately attempt to prolong body, existence, and visual relevancy.

But it's not just the sedation of age; it's also a perspective on living. Many of those who fight to preserve their youth seem to have lost their excitement for the future, and instead, appear to be in a constant effort of trying to get back to some time in their past. This may be the catalyst for the mid-life crisis or having affairs or plastic surgery or dressing like you did when you drove a Volkswagen Bug.

However, there is something to be said about a person who embraces their age. A man or woman content with the natural aging of his or her body. A person who has hope even in the face of death.

Ultimately, there is nothing wrong with maintaining a youthful spirit. There isn't anything inappropriate about maintaining your health. But there is something unfitting about a person who strives to reverse what is natural to the human experience.

As I mentioned above, the digitizing of our world is partly to blame. Computers have come to rule the marketplace and our homes, and millennials are the first generation to have been using them since birth. As a result, young people are now "smarter" than old people, which is certainly a first. A toddler can teach her aunt how to use her iPhone, and a middle-schooler has to help his grandfather set up an e-mail account.

Two hundred years ago, older people were always smarter than younger people. If you were born into a blacksmith family in the 1800s, your father always knew more about the craft than you. By the time you reached the age of twenty, he was in his third or even fourth decade in the craft. While you may be inventive, his extent of knowledge eclipsed your innovation. However, the Internet has reversed this situation.

Some of the smartest people on earth today are in their twenties and thirties. Magazines publish lists of innovators (for example, "30 Under 30" or "40 Under 40") who are barely out of college and already revolutionizing the world. The leading thinkers of our time include relatively young people like Mark Zuckerberg, who was born one year before I was in 1984.

But don't confuse smarter with wiser. That's one dynamic that will never change. Wisdom is the application of knowledge, and the more years you've accumulated, the more chances you've had to apply knowledge in the real world. The real question is whether you prefer smarter and savvier over wiser and more rational.

You might not be shocked to discover that the Bible prefers wisdom every time. It says that wisdom is more valuable than silver or gold. And because it is so valuable, old age is an asset rather than a liability. The Bible treats older people as wellsprings of wisdom that should be cherished and consulted. How did culture pervert this so completely?

Culture says that gray hair should be hidden under hair dye. Solomon said, "Gray hair is a crown of glory."[2]

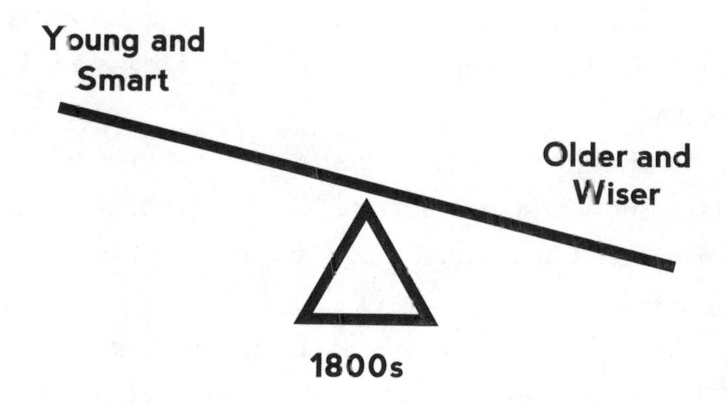
Young and
Smart
Older and
Wiser
1800s

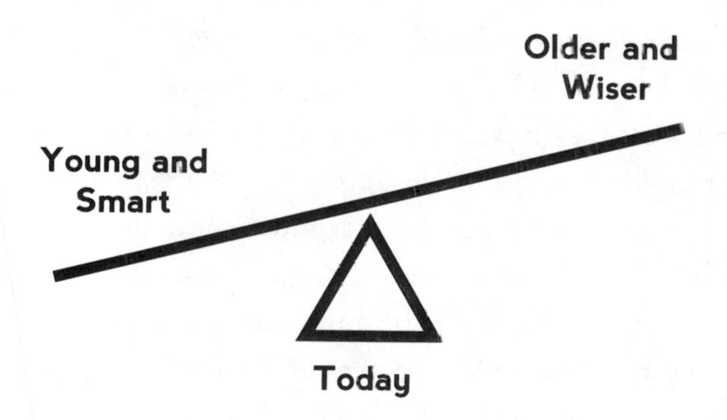
Older and
Wiser
Young and
Smart
Today

Our culture says that young people are gifted and have the most to contribute to society. But in Isaiah 3:12, God cursed Israel with young leaders. In Ecclesiastes 10:16, Solomon mocked cultures "whose king is a lad" (NASB).

Our culture says your best days are your younger days. But Ecclesiastes 7:10 says, "Say not, 'Why were the former days better than these?' For it is not from wisdom that you ask this" (ESV).

When I was terminated from the company I founded, I received a great deal of advice from peers. Clichés about God closing doors and opening windows abounded. I was peppered with e-mails that said, "Everything happens for a reason" and "It's always darkest before the dawn." These were intelligent people able to launch a business or design a beautiful website. But what they lacked is what I craved. I was desperate for understanding, for wisdom, and for direction.

At the time, I was living without community. As a result, I had nobody close enough who could console me. Nobody qualified to bear this burden. So I did what many community-less people do: I paid for it. I paid more than ten thousand dollars to sit under the apprenticeship of Dr. John Townsend: a Christian man in his late fifties, a world-renowned executive psychologist,

CULTURE SAYS:

~~Getting older is depressing.~~

WHAT GOD HAS TAUGHT ME:

Getting older is a blessing.

and one of the wisest men I know. He has a good reputation, a fruitful marriage, and has raised responsible children.

But could he help me—a man so broken and shattered and hurt? I had a running inventory of past afflictions so large it had stunted my effectiveness and ability to thrive. I was paralyzed by fear, unable to make decisions. I needed someone who had lived enough Christian life to help me separate my emotions from the truth in the Bible. Someone who was qualified to apply Scripture to my experience. Someone who had been to the valley and knew the way out. If anyone could guide me forward, it would be him.

Each month I spent eight hours at his house. I didn't know where to begin, but he did. I didn't know what to say, but he did. I didn't know how to feel, but he made me feel. We would often role-play, putting me into awkward situations, awakening past trauma, and training me how to react in future situations. Sometimes I would sob uncontrollably after he spoke. It turned out to be a year of healing, and I remember our last meeting as I sat on John's back porch, thinking, *No one my age could have done this for me.*

John embraced his age. He wore a suit. He wasn't flashy or flamboyant. He was comfortable in who he

If you want to be
successful, show
the world your age,
not your youth.

—DALE PARTRIDGE

was and wasn't trying to be someone else. And that is what made him a perfect mentor for me during that time. We need more John Townsends in the world, not more counterfeit adults.

As leaders, we should be seeking out the wisdom of age. We should be encouraging those who are older to embrace their time. We must be skeptical of modernism, and as the Bible says, "Ask for the old paths, where the good way is, and walk in it; then you will find rest for your souls."[3]

If you want to be successful, show the world your age, not your youth. If you want to move quickly, walk slowly. But most of all, if you want to be wise, celebrate the elderly. Embrace their pace. Care for their position in culture, because one day that position will be yours.

The Golden Calf

It's clear: culture's distorted definition of success will leave you vacant, broken, and washing up against the rocks of an empty glass.

However, let this book be a sword. A piece of truth warring against an enemy disguised as a friend. Let it be the eyes you need to find yourself. The ears required to hear the code.

Oblivion is the way of the wide. Its burden is a feather of iron. But truth always comes at the cost of change, growth, and resistance.

I'd like to close this book by exploring the concept of maturity.

I've defined *maturity* as "choosing to walk in godly character traits that are not natural to your personality."

Maturity is choosing to
walk in godly character
traits that are not natural
to your personality.

—DALE PARTRIDGE

In other words, conforming our flesh, our mind, our emotions, and our hearts to the Word of God.

Unlike most of our growth, maturity is detached from age. Meaning it is very possible to be physically mature while remaining spiritually immature.

I hope it's clear that this book's wisdom was not my own, but God's. I hope it's evident that my maturity was backed by the Scriptures and not by the intelligence of this world, for I have merely extrapolated the ideas of the Bible and translated them into a unique format.

Having said that, the only way your journey can continue beyond this book is in your ability to discern the truth on your own. Second Timothy 2:15 tells Christians to "be diligent to present yourself approved to God, a worker who does not need to be ashamed, rightly dividing the word of truth."

Paul's command here leaves us with three elements I'd like to unpack: diligence, shame, and the act of rightly dividing.

1. Diligence

Sadly, the newest trend among Christians is not diligence but neglecting of the Word of God. Christians who call

Jesus "Lord" but have eliminated Him from the arrangement of their days. Christians who are too tired for church, too occupied to open their Bibles, and too burnt out to pray. Instead, these followers of Christ opt for busy—the drug of choice for millions in today's culture. But it is the excuse of "busy" that sits between them and their spiritual maturity. It is "busy" that prohibits them from attaining the wisdom required to navigate today's spiritual landscape. Essentially, Christians lacking the diligence to read their Bible each day are Christians supporting the assistance of their own spiritual fall. A. W. Tozer so brilliantly said, "To have found God and still to pursue Him is the soul's paradox of love."[1] Saved by God and success with God are wildly different postures. Success requires pursuit. Success requires an unquenchable striving to seek even after He has been found. Diligence is the floor for such a relationship to be built. Without it, Paul knew the Christian would remain as he is: saved but not successful.

2. Shame

Shame is defined as "a painful feeling of humiliation or distress caused by the consciousness of wrong or foolish behavior."[2] Shame is not God's desire for His children. In fact, walking free of condemnation through the perfect sacrifice of Jesus, the repentance of our sin, and our obedience to God's Word allows us to stand approved and unashamed before God the Father. In Ephesians 5:8–19 Paul furthers God's desire by making a sincere call for Christians to walk righteously and avoid the shameful activities of darkness. In Hebrews 12:1–2, he commands us to "lay aside the sin that so easily entangles us"—a command to take hold of the freedom we have to be compliant to God's instructions. That being said, habitual, recurring sin is not part of the unashamed Christian life. It is not part of the journey God desires for you. Sure, repentance is available to all who sin, but there is a big difference between the person who every hundred miles slips and falls into the mud puddle, and the person who stops at the mud puddle, decides to stay there, and continues to jump back in day after day.

A worker who "does not need to be ashamed" is someone who walks free from the bondage of sin. Through Christ we are no longer victims to sin but victors over it. In Romans 8:37 it says we are "more than conquerors through Him who loved us." In 1 Corinthians 10:13 it says, "No temptation has overtaken you except such as is common to man; but God is faithful, who will not allow you to be tempted beyond what you are able, but with the temptation will also make the way of escape, that you may be able to bear it." God has made a way for us to win every single time. While sin is the founder of shame, Paul is reminding us that through the power of the Holy Spirit we can choose not to sin. We can choose not to have shame. But most of all, through Jesus, we can choose to walk in such a manner that our Lord deems us righteous, loved, and approved.

3. Rightly Dividing

We're going to camp here for a moment. Rightly dividing implies the contrasting concept of wrongly dividing, and unfortunately, we can wrongly divide the Word of Truth. In my opinion we have a theological epidemic on our hands. We have many churches and many Christians who will do just about anything to escape the authority of difficult or unpopular Scripture verses.

Over the past several years, I've heard countless pastors dance around politically charged topics and cleverly use phrases like, "Remember, this isn't a letter to us but to the Corinthians . . ." or "What this scripture is *really* saying is . . ." Or my personal vexation:

"Be mindful that these were instructions for people more than two thousand years ago . . ." To which I often respond with, "The Jews of Jesus' day never reduced the authority of Scripture from Moses or the Old Testament because of when they were written. But somehow the jurisdiction of the New Testament is reduced because of its antiquity. Sounds suspicious to me."

The reality is, the Bible is becoming hate speech to the culture. There's a reason it's outlawed or regulated in dozens of countries across the globe. There's a reason many pastors have chosen to operate within a topical teaching regimen where an entire sermon can revolve around one or two positive and uplifting scriptures. The truth is offensive (1 Corinthians 1:18).

However, successful Christians must approach and preach the Word of God with boldness, without fear, without flaw, and as inerrant and authoritative. Second Timothy 3:14–17 says,

> But you must continue in the things which you have learned and been assured of, knowing from whom you have learned them, and that from childhood you have known the Holy Scriptures, which are able to make you wise for salvation through faith which is in Christ Jesus.

> All Scripture is given by inspiration of God, and is profitable for doctrine, for reproof, for correction, for instruction in righteousness, that the man [or woman] of God may be complete, thoroughly equipped for every good work.

Now, we must approach Scripture with wisdom. We must recognize the difference between prescription and description. We must understand context, audience, and authorship. But when books like 1 Corinthians, for example, open with an audience address that says, "To the church of God which is at Corinth, to those who are sanctified in Christ Jesus, called to be saints, with *all* who in *every* place call on the name of Jesus Christ our Lord, both theirs and ours,"[3] we must ask ourselves, "Are we the church of God who is at Corinth?" No. "Are we those who are sanctified in Christ Jesus?" Yes. "Are we called to be saints?" Yes. "Are we a part of the 'all who in every place call on the name of Jesus Christ our Lord'?" Yes. Did Paul tell us when this letter would lose its authority in the lives of Christians? No. Are we willing to guess that maybe after 300 years it was no longer relevant? What about 500 years? Maybe 735 years? I hope you're seeing my point. Even though this letter speaks to several matters specific to the Corinthian church, Paul intended this epistle to be the general property of the universal church of Christ. Whether that was the church of ancient Ephesus or Rome or modern California or England, this book still holds its dominion. While this is only one example from one book in the Bible, it is important to recognize these subtleties as you continue your journey of rightly dividing God's truth.

Ultimately, in a culture that seems to be moving further from God's Word, we must ask ourselves, "Who moved? Us or Him?" Second Timothy 4:3–4 says,

> For the time will come when they will not endure sound doctrine, but according to their own desires, because they have itching ears, they will heap up for themselves teachers; and they will turn their ears away from the truth, and be turned aside to fables.

Christians, success in this world must come from a firm, unwavering practice of filling our souls with God's truth. We must be more concerned with being biblically correct than politically correct. We must be enthusiastic to please our God, not our fellow man.

As you journey through the valley of life, you will be presented with counterfeits and reproductions. You will be wooed toward false wells of hope. You will watch many people drown in their own paths, and you will mourn for them.

The word *success* has been hijacked by the culture. We have reduced it, twisted it, and molded it into a golden calf for society to worship. If you're not careful, you'll find yourself on your knees before an idol: a lifestyle chasing everything your God is against.

Today's definition of success is a form of godliness without the power. It is something to guard against. It is something to fear. It is something to be saved from.

+ Finishing Well

As many of you know, this generation doesn't have a knowledge problem. We have a consumption problem. We're addicted to learning for the sake of knowing. Book after book. Podcast after podcast. Conference after conference. Sermon after sermon. But still, for many of us, life remains the same. Sin still lives on. Hearts remain unmoved. Lives stay static. It reveals something quite tragic: a love affair with idleness.

If we're going to be honest with ourselves, we don't hate growth. We hate change. We hate discipline. We hate the work required to put our flesh in subjection to our spirit.

James 1:22–25 says,

> But be doers of the word, and not hearers only, deceiving yourselves. For if anyone is a hearer of the word and not a doer, he is like a man observing his natural face in a mirror; for he observes himself, goes away, and immediately forgets what kind of man he was. But he who looks into the perfect law of liberty and continues in it, and is not a forgetful hearer but a doer of the work, this one will be blessed in what he does.

What a tragedy it would be if this book had simply become another piece of content to consume. How sad it would be to see these lessons abandoned—never to be translated into anything except further knowledge.

That is not my heart for you. For that reason, I have produced a comprehensive application study guide for individuals and groups who have completed this book and are looking for more. A beautifully designed digital resource to help you convert the more challenging areas of this written work into deep maturity, change, and spiritual growth.

To download a copy for yourself or your small group simply visit SavedFromSucess.com/StudyGuide.

Lastly, if you believe this content could add value to other people in your Christian community, consider leading others through a *Saved from Success* group study or having me speak at your next gathering, church service, or event.

To a life toward the narrow gate,

Dale Partridge

Dale.Partridge@UnlearnChurch.org

Acknowledgments

God, thank you for a larger portion. Thank you for revealing yourself in miraculous ways. May I serve you until my very last breath.

Veronica, you are an ocean of joy that I do not deserve. Thank you for your willingness to follow me into battle or beauty.

Aria, your little heart is a huge contributor to my journey. Thank you for your love, your hugs, and your smile.

Honor and Valor, thank you for calling my name while I'm writing. It is a lovely reminder to stop working.

Matt, you are an instrument of the Lord. Thank you for representing Him well.

Aaron, thank you for your wisdom and thinking of the title of this book.

Chris, thanks for following along. Many leave, the strong stay.

About the Author

Dale Partridge is the founder and editor in chief of UnlearnChurch.org, a *Wall Street Journal* bestselling author, and advocate for biblical church. With over 500,000 followers on social media and 500,000 monthly readers of his blog, Dale is a provocative influencer on the topics of church, family, manhood, and marriage. He is a trusted advisor to a variety of Christian publications and his work has been featured on Fox News, NBC, *Christianity Today, The Today Show, Good Morning America, Faithwire*, and *The Huffington Post.* Dale and his wife reside with their three children on their farm in Central Oregon.

Notes

Chapter 00: Succeeding at Failing

1. "Definition of *success*, Oxford Dictionaries, accessed December 31, 2017, https://en.oxforddictionaries.com/definition/us/success.
2. "Synonyms for *success*," Oxford Dictionaries Thesaurus, accessed November 30, 2017, https://en.oxforddictionaries.com/thesaurus/success.
3. 1 Corinthians 3:18–19.
4. 1 Corinthians 10:12.

Chapter 01: Marriage

1. D'vera Cohn, "Marriage Rate Declines and Marriage Age Rises," Pew Research Center, December 14, 2011, http://www.pewsocialtrends.org/2011/12/14/marriage-rate-declines-and-marriage-age-rises/.
2. Genesis 2:18, emphasis added.
3. Genesis 2:24–25, emphasis added.
4. R. Albert Mohler Jr., "The Case for (Early) Marriage," *Christian Post*, August 3, 2009, http://www.christianpost.com/news/the-case-for-early-marriage-40059/.

5. Gary Thomas, *Sacred Marriage: What If God Designed Marriage to Make Us Holy More Than to Make Us Happy?* (Grand Rapids: Zondervan, 2015), 11.
6. Lori Hollander, "Five Truths Every Married Person Needs to Know About Affairs," Good Therapy, July 21, 2011, https://www.goodtherapy.org/blog/truths-workplace-affair/.
7. 1 Peter 5:8.
8. Ephesians 5:25.
9. Ephesians 5:22.

Chapter 02: Children

1. Jillian Kramer, "One-Third of Millennials Don't Want Kids," *Glamour*, October 22, 2015, http://www.glamour.com/story/millennials-dont-want-kids.
2. Psalm 127:3 NIV.
3. Proverbs 17:6 NIV.
4. Psalm 127:5 NIV.
5. Genesis 1:22.
6. Andy Stanley (@AndyStanley), "Your greatest contribution to the kingdom of God may not be something you do but someone you raise," Twitter, April 17, 2013, 9:38 p.m., https://twitter.com/andystanley/status/324713440541290498.

Chapter 03: Money

1. Psalm 62:10.
2. Mark 4:19.
3. Luke 16:14.
4. Suzanne Woolley, "Do You Have More Debt Than the Average American?" Bloomberg, December 15, 2016, https://www

.bloomberg.com/news/articles/2016-12-15/average-credit-card-debt-16k-total-debt-133k-where-do-you-fit-in.

5. Matthew 25:21.
6. John Townsend, *The Entitlement Cure: Finding Success in Doing Hard Things the Right Way* (Grand Rapids: Zondervan, 2015).

Chapter 04: Purpose

1. Brad Lomenick, *H3 Leadership: Be Humble. Stay Hungry. Always Hustle.* (Nashville: Nelson Books, 2015), 54.

Chapter 05: Influence

1. Proverbs 22:1.

Chapter 06: Freedom

1. Proverbs 18:1.
2. Galatians 6:2.
3. James 5:16.

Chapter 07: Youth

1. Tom Winterbottom, "Stanford Literary Scholar Traces Cultural History of Our Obsession with Youth," *Stanford Report*, November 19, 2014, http://news.stanford.edu/news/2014/november/youthful-book-harrison-111914.html.
2. Proverbs 16:31 ESV.
3. Jeremiah 6:16.

The Golden Calf

1. A. W. Tozer, *The Pursuit of God* (Abbotsford, WI: Aneko Press, 2015), 4.

2. "Shame," Oxford Living Dictionaries, accessed December 4, 2017, https://en.oxforddictionaries.com/definition/shame.
3. 1 Corinthians 1:2 NIV.

Millions of Christians are leaving the church on a search for Jesus.

UnlearnChurch.org

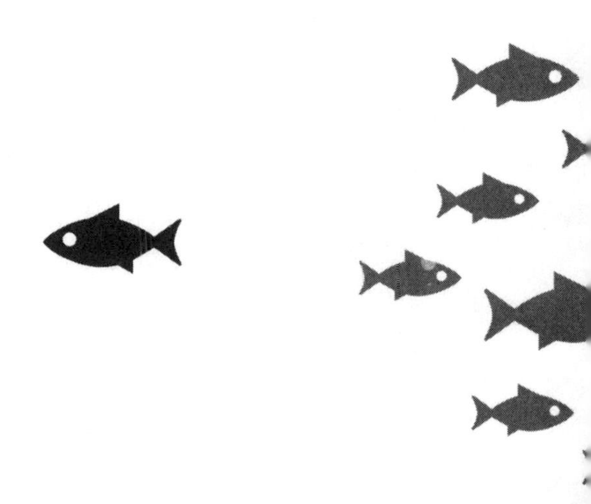

THE NEW BLOG OF "*SAVED FROM SUCCESS*" AUTHOR, DALE PARTRIDGE

Learn how to plant a biblical house church.

RelearnChurch.org

A 3-DAY WORKSHOP WITH DALE PARTRIDGE